**THEY MADE
TYNESIDE
GREAT**

About the author

John Sadler was born and raised on Tyneside, was educated in the region and has always worked in the Newcastle upon Tyne area. He is married with two daughters and lives in Belsay in mid Northumberland and his previous published works include *Battle for Northumbria* (Bridge Studios, 1988) and *Scottish Battles* (Canongate, 1994). He practises law with a leading Newcastle firm and has been involved in providing help and guidance to small businesses for the past decade. He is a member of a number of local history societies and lectures regularly to general and special interest groups.

Project North East is an independent, but non-profit, local enterprise and economic development agency whose purpose is to develop and implement innovative economic solutions which will offer individuals and organisations the opportunity to realise their potential.

It aims to achieve this through assisting people who want to start their own business as well as people already in business who have the aspiration and potential to grow.

In August 1992, Project North East took a lease on Hawthorn House, a building which has seen many pioneering efforts in the industrial development of Newcastle. The land on which Hawthorn House is built was left by Thomas Horsley, one of the Merchant Adventurers, to the St Mary the Virgin Trust.

"The Merchant Adventurers of Newcastle upon Tyne"

Project North East's re-development of Hawthorn House attracted considerable sponsorship from the private and public sectors and from the European Community. This book is intended both to describe some of Newcastle's early pioneers and to thank all of the sponsors each of whom has chosen to be linked to an individual pioneer.

Special thanks are due to ESSO who not only contributed to the building development but also sponsored this book.

THEY MADE TYNESIDE GREAT

by
John Sadler

Copyright © Project North East 1994

ISBN: 1-85557-006-8

First Published 1994 by Project North East,
Hawthorn House, Forth Banks, Newcastle upon Tyne, NE1 3SG.

In association with
Pandon Press, P.O. Box ISN, Newcastle upon Tyne, NE99 1SN.

Acknowledgements

The pictures in this book have been reproduced by kind permission of the following (the numbers refer to pages):

Beamish North of England Open Air Museum, County Durham: 38.
British Gas, Scotland: 21.
Newcastle upon Tyne Central Library: 15,17, 18, 20, 23, 24, 26, 27, 29, 30, 33, 37, 41, 43, 45.
Tyne & Wear Archives Service, by permission of the Chief Archivist: 11.
Tyne & Wear Museums Service: 35.
From the collection of the Laing Art Gallery: front cover, 6, 32.
Procter & Gamble: 39.
Reyrolle Limited: 47.
Royal Grammar School: 13.

Printed in Great Britain by Colden Offset Ltd., Cowen Road, Blaydon-on-Tyne, Tyne & Wear, NE21 5TW.

CONTENTS

Panoramic View of Newcastle in 1893, looking south, (from a watercolour by Joseph Skelton).

The birth of industrial Newcastle

Newcastle's formidable medieval walls, which withstood a famous siege by the Army of the Solemn League and Covenant in 1644 remained intact until as late as 1745 when they were last prepared for defence against the Young Pretender. After that, sections of masonry began to be demolished and the modern city was born.

The latter half of the 1700s saw a gradual movement away from the traditional heart of the city, clustered around The Close and Sandhill, with the new houses of the gentry being built in Pilgrim Street and along Westgate Road. New, elegant houses in the Georgian manner sprang up in Charlotte Square near Blackfriars and outside the line of the ancient walls; new houses were being built in Lower Northumberland Street, backed by extensive gardens, and the elegant terraces of Saville Place and Saville Row were completed around 1788.

At this stage in the city's history, before the railways, horsedrawn traffic which crawled over the old Tyne Bridge had to pull up the tortuous rise of The Side to reach the upper town. The flash flood, which occurred on 17 November 1771, swept away the old bridge almost as though heralding the birth of the Georgian cityscape. Between 1784 and 1789 the rancorous open sewer of the Lort Burn was filled in and the lower reaches of Dean Street were built over. At the head of Dean Street a new lateral thoroughfare, Mosley Street, was constructed to join Pilgrim Street to the main centre of town. A Theatre Royal was built in Mosley Street in 1788 and in 1810 the street was extended by the addition of Collingwood Street to join on to Westgate Road. These new streets were built in the crisp simplicity of the classical manner, their lower storeys ornamented by rows of fashionable shops.

In 1796 the architect and builder, David Stephenson, completed his masterpiece, the new All Saints' Church and, between the years 1795 and 1811, all of the gates of the medieval town were pulled down, save Newgate, which survived until 1823.

Improvements during the Georgian era were not restricted to the purely architectural and environmental. There was a general move toward cultural and social enlightenment and by 1802 Newcastle had no fewer than five newspapers including the oldest, the *Newcastle Courant* which had begun printing in 1712. Throughout the latter part of the 18th century the city became a centre of printing and publishing, culminating in the superb illustrations of Thomas Bewick. Growing prosperity and the increase of mercantile trade fuelled the growth of a new class of urban bourgeoisie which in turn led to the foundation of a number of private schools with various humanitarian and medical societies. In 1793 the Literary and Philosophical Society was formed, followed in 1813 by the Society of Antiquaries.

This increase in prosperity was paralleled by a rapid growth in population and, by the end of the century, the city was home to some 28,000 people. The poorer of these were accommodated in a sprawl of insanitary slums clustered around the lanes and chares of Sandgate and the Quayside. Even after the major rebuilding carried out by Grainger and Dobson in the early 19th century the Quayside area remained almost untouched and the squalor was fuelled by the arrival of waves of Scottish and Irish immigrants who brought with them typhus, scarlet fever and, most devastating, cholera epidemics which swept the city in 1831 and again in 1853. Only a massive explosion on the Gateshead side of the river in 1854, which erupted like divine fury and levelled large areas of the Quayside, provided the opportunity for rebuilding.

In the 1830s, the thrusting entrepreneur and builder Richard Grainger formed a partnership with the talented architect John Dobson and the highly competent town clerk and solicitor John Clayton. It is an interesting reflection on Victorian civic morality that Clayton apparently saw no conflict of interest in his dual role of town clerk and as solicitor to the developer — nor, apparently, did any of his contemporaries feel that such a contradictory mix of obligations was inappropriate. Grainger bought a derelict, 12-acre site between Pilgrim Street and Newgate Street which was to form the nucleus for his new town development. Previously, he had built Higham Place (1819-20), Eldon Square and Blackett Street (1824-26), and Leazes Terrace (1829-34). Between 1831 and 1832 he constructed the Royal Arcade in Pilgrim Street.

Obviously there was little harm done in having the town clerk, who was effectively chief executive of the local authority, on the development team and there can be no doubt that this helped to push Grainger's ambitious redevelopment scheme past the City Fathers. The Dobson/Grainger masterpiece saw the construction of upper Dean Street (now Grey Street), Grainger Street and Clayton Street. As well as having a fine, classical style, the buildings were fully equipped with modern sewerage and sanitation, something of a revelation for the period.

As a result, the distinguished architectural historian Niklaus Pevsner says of Newcastle that it is, 'the best designed Victorian town in England and indeed the best designed large city in England altogether.'

It was part of the Dobson/Grainger concept that Grey Street, together with Dean Street, would remain the main commercial thoroughfare. In fact this intention was disturbed within a decade by the development of the railway in 1849. The subsequent construction of the Central Station and the High Level Bridge shifted attention away from Grainger's axis and virtually cut off the Quayside area which had, hitherto, been the traditional commercial heart of the city.

The Victorian era became one of unprecedented economic and social change. Industrialisation on a scale undreamt of was accompanied by a substantial explosion in the size of population. The development of the south east Northumberland Coalfield led to a rash of new towns and villages springing up within the area. Nonetheless, by 1840 a number of Newcastle's traditional industries were in irreversible decline. Although coal mining itself continued to develop, fuelled by the growth of the railways and a growing demand for steam coal, the collier trade was seriously threatened by the new railways. The iron industry was decimated by developments in Cleveland and the heart of the iron trade shifted from the Tyne to the Tees.

The glass and alkali industries which had been traditional staples of the Newcastle economy also declined through competition from Cleveland. The state of the Tyne continued to remain an inhibiting factor, but in 1850 the river became the responsibility of the Tyne Improvement Commission who gradually carried out dredging and improvement works; perhaps their most spectacular achievement was the building of the Swing Bridge which opened in 1876. The coal industry boosted the growth of small ports strung along the North East coast such as Blyth which, in 1860, was able to ship only some 25,000 tons of coal a year, but by 1913 was shipping up to 4,750,000 tons annually.

The 19th century witnessed a wealth of design and entrepreneurial talent which can scarcely have been equalled in history. A generation of men existed, whose genius was matched only by their business acumen, whose achievement effectively moulded the course of the region's future and whose heritage, at least in part, remains with us today. One of the first of these was Charles Mark Palmer who began life as a coal owner and who designed and constructed a steam propelled iron ship to meet the competition of the railways which were killing off the traditional collier trade. He designed the vessel *John Bowes* which went down the slipway in 1852. The new craft immediately proved its worth and was able to deliver as much coal to London in a five day return trip as a timber built collier would have achieved in two months. Palmer's Jarrow yard was soon turning out iron ships to order and the great era of North East shipbuilding had begun.

William George Armstrong was the son of a Newcastle corn merchant and former Lord Mayor. He began his career as a solicitor but soon gave up practising law in order to pursue his interest in engineering design. His earliest creation was the hydraulic crane and he began manufacturing on a site in Elswick in 1867. Mid-Victorian wars gave him his greatest opportunity and his breech-loading field gun revolutionised the science of artillery. His factory, which employed 30 men when it first opened in the mid-19th century was, by 1900, employing over 25,000.

Tyneside's reputation was built on a history of manufacturing and design excellence exemplified by such household names as Hawthorn Leslie, Swan Hunter, Clarke Chapman and CA Parsons. At the Spithead naval review of 1897 Parsons amazed the mandarins of the Royal Navy when his steam turbine driven vessel *Turbinia* weaved in and out of the mighty dreadnaughts at an almost unbelievable speed of 30 knots. Parsons later developed the Turbo Alternator for electric power and Tyneside became one of the important suppliers to the early electrical industry. The crowning achievement of this remarkable era was the launch of the great liner *Mauretania*, built by Swans in 1906 and powered by Parsons' turbines.

This surge in industrial development was complemented by further rapid growth in population. The rustic village of Elswick expanded from a population of 3,539 in 1851 to 27,800 in less than two decades.

By 1871, two fifths of Newcastle's population was born outside of the counties of Northumberland and Durham, 30 per cent were of Scottish origin and 19 per cent Irish. Despite the dreadful poverty which was prevalent throughout the early years of the century, housing standards were gradually improving. The now familiar terraces of back-to-back houses were constructed in great numbers in the latter part of the century. The old medieval city finally disappeared and the modern urban sprawl, its skyline punctuated by a framework of shipyard cranes, was born.

The story of Forth Banks

The development of Newcastle from medieval township to industrialised conurbation was perhaps nowhere more telling than in the area which lay to the west of the city walls. In the stone walling there was a postern gate, set some ten yards east of the Neville Tower which gave access to open ground beyond, simply called *Without the Wall*. This open ground led on to the *Frith* or *Forth*, an ancient common situated next to the hospital of St. Mary the Virgin. The ground covered by the common probably lay between what is now the west end of Forth Lane and the top of Forth Banks, most of it being covered by Forth Goods Station.

In ancient times it is possible that *Le Frythe* comprised a sacred grove of oaks associated with the Celtic Druidic cult though, whilst intriguing, this is largely speculative. The area is first mentioned in the reign of Henry III when the townsmen were licensed to dig for coals and stone in return for an annual rental of one mark. The subsequent grant to the burgesses, who were effectively the freemen of the city and who controlled trade in the area was made, at a Fee Farm rent by Edward III apparently as a reward for sterling service by the townsmen in repulsing an attack by the Scots. The burgesses continued to pay their £4 a year for the 11 acres certainly until 1649, though there is evidence from the period of the Protectorate that the rather informal recreational use was extended and formalised with the laying down of a bowling green. Subsequently the park was developed and walled and for many years the

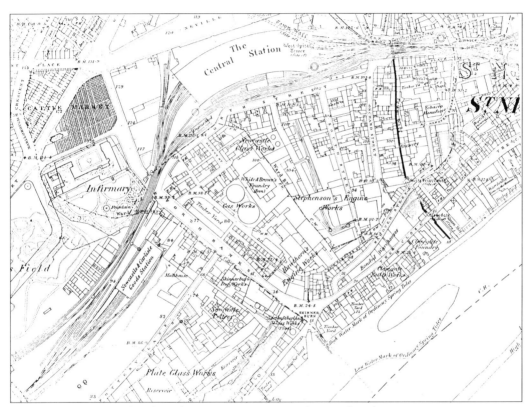

Map of Forth Banks area (TWAS OS 1st edn 25 inch scale XCV11.7).

mayor, sheriff and aldermen participated in an ancient custom when they, together with the townspeople, celebrated the Feasts of Easter and Whitsuntide upon the Forth.

In April 1751, a group of professional men, led by Mr. Richard Lambert, a surgeon, opened a subscription in Newcastle for the building of a general infirmary and fitted out a house in Gallowgate for the reception of patients whilst the monies were gathered in. The Corporation, mindful perhaps of Forth Banks' history as an ancient hospital site, offered a parcel of land to the subscribers at a nominal rent.

Building work began in September of the same year, and on 8 October of the following year, the new hospital opened with 90 beds. Eight years later the number of surgeons was doubled from two to four. To celebrate the centenary of the foundation a new wing was built in 1852, and the institution later benefited from substantial endowments from both Lord Armstrong and George Stephenson.

Nonetheless the hospital became increasingly cramped and isolated as foot, railway and cattle traffic increased throughout the area. The Diamond Jubilee of Queen Victoria was chosen as the occasion to raise a further £100,000 by subscription for a new infirmary which in turn led to the construction of what is now the Royal Victoria Infirmary, opened by the monarch on 11 July 1906.

At the beginning of the 19th century the Forth district still retained much of its old and semi-rural appearance. Outside the town wall, beside Hanover Square, a row of gardens and orchards stretched from the White Friars' Tower to the Postern. The memory of these lost gardens still lingers on in the name of Orchard Street which is built on the site. From the Postern a track led to the bowling green which was apparently separated by hedgerows from the green fields and gardens on the other side. Forth Banks itself ran up from Skinnerburn Mouth past the potteries in Pottery Lane and past the infirmary; the bowling green stood at the top on the right hand side with its rows of lime trees and low brick wall still to the fore.

The 19th century observer McKenzie, writing in 1827, noted that the balcony at Forth House provided an excellent vantage 'from whence the spectators, calmly smoking their pipes and enjoying their glasses, beheld the sportsmen'. He observed both decline and later improvement in the area noting, "it was let out in tenements and the trees had become much decayed and the beauty of the green much defaced by the constant exercising of troops but this is now stopped; the place is put in order and young trees planted. It is the most delightful and convenient promenade in the vicinity of the town".

By the early 19th century, however, the character of the area was due to change irrevocably. In 1824 Stephenson opened his railway workshop in Forth Street, followed by Hawthorn three years later. Armstrong bought two fields in the pretty village of Elswick as a site for his factory. The establishment of these three businesses heralded the true birth of heavy engineering on Tyneside.

Thomas Horsley
1462 - 1544

The age of the Merchant Adventurers

Though born into the high middle ages, Thomas Horsley belongs in the Renaissance — a new man, a man of commerce rather than of iron, a trader rather than a warrior or priest.

Horsley is justly famed as the founder of the Newcastle Grammar School and was described in his day as a 'merchant adventurer'. He was Mayor of Newcastle on no less than six occasions and, like so many of his contemporaries, he benefited extensively from the dissolution of the monasteries under Henry VIII in 1535 and 1536, acquiring extensive dominican possessions at Bamburgh.

Thomas Horsley was born the year after the Wars of the Roses reached their bloody height at the battle of Towton in Yorkshire when the Yorkists, under the young King Edward IV, massively defeated their Lancastrian rivals led, at least in name, by the old King Henry VI. The wars spluttered on in the North for a further three years until the final definitive rout of the Lancastrians at Hexham Levels in 1464.

The coming of the 16th century brought with it a whole new set of ideas, heavily influenced by continental models. The old order of feudal chivalry, which had reigned supreme throughout the shires, was being challenged by a new urban meritocracy, men who owed their fortunes not to favour or lineage but to trade — men such as Thomas Horsley. One of the reasons for their success was a tax loophole.

Throughout the middle ages, the county of Northumberland had remained almost entirely pastoral and the city and port of Newcastle had formed the focus for the export of grindstones, hides, wool and coal. In the 13th century, Newcastle was exporting more hides than any other port in the country and, by the middle of the following century, some 500 sacks of wool a year. Both Newcastle and its northern, (formerly Scottish) neighbour, Berwick had enjoyed the benefit of a special royal licence which

empowered them to export northern wool free of all duty direct to the Netherlands. The less-principled producers from the south sent their wool to Newcastle for onward shipment to avoid the duty. Newcastle gained a lucrative benefit from its privilege.

As the 15th century wore on, the export of coal became increasingly important. The coal industry in the region was very much in its infancy. Though surface workings had been established by the 14th century, they were only gradually replaced by galleried pits. Most of these early pits were on church lands giving the clergy a virtual monopoly on the mining of coal, but there was a snag: although the coal might come from monastic lands, the Prince Bishop and others were still dependant upon the burgesses of Tyneside to export the raw material. So the later middle ages saw an almost constant power struggle between the burgesses and the clergy — a struggle not decided until the reformation.

Before the great upheaval resulting from Henry VIII's failure to obtain a papal annulment of his marriage to Catherine of Aragon, both the Prince Bishop and the Prior of Tynemouth had been the most powerful clerical magnates in the infant coal industry. The burgesses, to consolidate their position and to line further their own purses, began to claim the right of 'hosting' merchant strangers. In practice, the burgesses would insist that a freeman of Newcastle had to be a party to every transaction with a visiting merchant. Thus, if a trader came to Newcastle wishing to exchange corn for coal he was obliged to sell to and buy from a burgess. Thus the coal merchants of Newcastle became Hostmen.

Horsley's achievements were considerable: in 1512 he was High Sheriff and a Commissioner of the peace for Northumberland; he became a Master of the Fellowship of Merchants, his own trade being corn chandler; in 1513, whilst an alderman, he accepted responsibility for the supply of horses to the Earl of Surrey's army which was on the march north to meet King James IV of Scotland.

On a wet September day in that year the English and Scottish armies clashed bloodily at Flodden. The Scottish army was decimated, their King slain. The next year Horsley was elected mayor and also Master of the Merchant Adventurers. When Horsley died he left substantial revenue in the form of a trust fund for the establishment of a grammar school, subsequently founded in 1545. His grammar or 'hyghe skull' was originally housed in a building in St. Nicholas' Churchyard until refounded as the free Grammar School of Queen Elizabeth by a charter in 1600.

It was possible for merchant adventurers, such as Horsley to amass vast fortunes. We can gain an insight into the life of a 16th century merchant adventurer from the will of William Jenison, who was Mayor of Newcastle in 1581. He left houses in Newcastle, Thorpe and Haswell with corn and cattle at Benwell, Woodcroft, Walworth, North Woodham, Thorpe, Haswell and Eden. He left a warehouse in The Close and leases of mines at Crossmoor, Fitburn Moor, Newbiggin and Holinside with coals lying wrought at 13 pits, a salt pan in Jarrow, three Keels, two lighters and a share in the 'Grand Lease', valued at £1,000 — a very significant sum for the period.

Lord Cuthbert Collingwood
1748 - 1810

Newcastle's hero of Trafalgar

The British Navy's proudest moment is probably still the Battle of Trafalgar. After its Commander in Chief, Lord Nelson, was killed at the height of the action, it was Newcastle's Lord Collingwood who took over command and secured victory.

He was born by the Quayside, the traditional heart of the city, in 1748. Although this area was in decline during the 18th century as many people of the wealthier classes sought to move away from the jumble of narrow chares, slums and shanties, the traditional pull of the Quayside, and particularly of Sandhill, kept many tradespeople living and working there.

Shops, warehouses, factories, coffee houses, jostled side by side. There was a daily market for fish and bread and on Tuesdays and Saturdays there was a market for cloth, leather and general goods. In one of these shops, with living quarters above, Cuthbert Collingwood was born and named after his father, who was one of those succesful tradesmen.

Young Cuthbert attended the Grammar School in Newcastle but, by the age of 11, he had already decided on a career at sea. Perhaps he was influenced by living on the Quayside where the constant passage of merchant shipping must have been a thrilling sight to a young boy with an adventurous spirit. Perhaps he chose the sea because his uncle by marriage was master of the *Shannon*. Perhaps, simply, his instincts told him that naval warfare was where his talents lay.

By 1774, he was serving under Vice-Admiral Graves having been highly recommended by his former master, Captain, later Admiral, J. Rodden, of the *Lennox*. He also seems to have made a very good impression on Admiral Graves and in 1775 he was to be found serving as Fourth Lieutenant on the *Somerset* where he had the unenviable distinction of being present at the disastrous and bloody battle of *Bunker Hill* when the British Redcoats took on the untrained levies of America's rebellious colonies.

ACTION FOR CITIES

After the debacle at Boston, he was transferred to the *Hornet* and was sent under orders to Jamaica where he was able to cement his relationship with another up and coming young star of the Navy, Horatio Nelson with whose career his own was to become inextricably bound. Indeed, it seemed for a while that Collingwood was destined to dog Nelson's footsteps as he became his replacement on the *Lowestoffe* when Nelson was promoted. Collingwood's next advancement was as post-captain on the *Badge*, and subsequently on the *Hinchinbrooke*, following his friend on both occasions.

He soon had his master's ticket, commanding both the *Pelican* and the *Samson*, and served in the West Indies until 1786 before returning to Tyneside where he remained ashore until 1790 when further hostilities with Spain threatened and he was nominated to take command of the *Mermaid*.

On 16 June 1791, he married Sarah, the eldest daughter of Alderman J.E. Blackett. This domestic idyll was short lived and he was soon back in service against the French. He distinguished himself in battle in an engagement now referred to as the glorious 1st of June where he commanded the *Barfleur*, but when Lord Howe reported on the action, he was mysteriously passed over, an omission or insult which appeared to rankle for some years.

Nonetheless Collingwood's naval achievements could not long be ignored and, in command of the *Excellent* , he was instrumental in winning the battle of Cape St. Vincent. Nelson was impressed, as always, by his friend's conduct and wrote to him: 'Dear Collingwood, a friend in need is a friend indeed.' Collingwood refused to accept the medal struck to commemorate the battle, still smarting from having been passed over after the earlier action. The Admiralty, now realising the error of its ways sent a medal for that fight together with an apology for its delay in transmission. The *Excellent* was paid off in January 1799 when Collingwood was gazetted a Rear Admiral of the White. Soon after he was promoted to Rear Admiral of the Red.

In 1805, Collingwood's finest hour arrived. On the most famous day in British naval history it was Collingwood who led the vanguard of the English Fleet into action and he was reported to have said to his officers as the first shots began to fall, 'Now gentlemen, let us do something today which the world may talk of hereafter'. His flagship the *Royal Sovereign* took as a prize the great Spanish battleship *Santa Anna*. When Nelson was shot down and mortally wounded the command passed automatically to him. Although credit for the plan of battle and its inception belong to Nelson, Collingwood certainly deserves his full share of the laurels for the masterful manner in which it was carried through despite the loss of the Commander in Chief. *'Who at the hour when Nelson died, With dauntless zeal the mighty loss supplied.'*

After the epic Battle of Trafalgar, Collingwood began to suffer increasingly from ill-health. He relinquished high command and died at sea on 7 March 1810.

Thomas Bewick
1753 - 1828

Turning engineering into an artform

Thomas Bewick is regarded as the father of wood engraving: he was born at Cherryburn, Northumberland, in an age when the industrialisation of the landscape was in its merest infancy. Although the development of the coalfields was beginning to gather pace, the Northumbrian landscape still retained a largely pastoral aspect, the city safe within walls that had been refurbished to meet the threat of the Jacobite risings.

Bewick showed a precocious talent at an early age which included his leaving chalk drawings on the doors of village houses — an expression of talent that was not necessarily appreciated by his contemporaries. At the age of 14, he was apprenticed to Beilby in Newcastle at his glassworks.

The glass industry was at this time well established and at the very height of its prosperity. Capital for the industry was provided by the burgesses and coal barons in the 17th century. The history of glass-making on Tyneside was, therefore, largely linked to the development of the coalfields. The growth in demand for glass came as glazed windows became more popular from the reign of Elizabeth onward. Glaziers were attracted by the availability of coal as cheap fuel and also a plentiful supply of sand brought as ballast by colliers. In 1619, Sir Robert Mansell had established a glassworks at the mouth of the Ouseburn at Byker and is said to have been the first to import Hugenot refugees from Lorraine who brought with them considerable glassworking skills. By 1740, Mansell's works had three furnaces, employed 60 people and was capable of producing 3,000 cases of glass each year. Tyneside became the principal source of window glass and, by 1772, there were some 16 glassworks, mostly located on the east Quayside, in the Ouseburn area beyond Sandgate.

Community Unit

Oak Tree with View of Newcastle (Thomas Bewick).

Whilst still an apprentice with Beilby, Bewick was approached by a Dr. Hutton, a leading mathematician about to publish a work upon mensuration; he had decided to illustrate his work with wood cuts, instead of the more conventional steel or copper engravings. This commission went to the young Bewick and defined the course of his future career. He illustrated several more works on mathematics but it was in the field of natural history and anthropology that his real interest lay.

Subsequently his wood cuts for *Gay's Fables, History of Quadrupeds* and *The History of British Bird*s established his reputation and his brilliant creations have not since been equalled. His wood cuts were supported by a series of sketches from life which are themselves a considerable artistic achievement.

Of his sketches of animals a contemporary writer was moved to say: 'A great and unexpected charm belonged to both the history of quadrupeds and of birds. This was the profusion of vinyets and tail pieces of which the volumes are adorned. Many of these happy little embellishments are connected with the manners and habits of the animals near which they are placed. Others again, merely exhibit the fancies and the humour of the artist, his particular notions of men and things partaking both of the droll and the pathetic; as for instance, a ragged, half-starved sheep picking at a besom; a group of Savoyards, weary and foot sore, tugging a poor bear to the near fair; a broken down soldier, slouching with stern patience through the slanting rain storm; a poor, travelling woman, looking wistfully at a mutilated milestone; the blind, old beggar, whose faithful dog stopped short, with warning whine, on the broken plank that should have crossed the swollen brook ... all delineatory of scenes true to nature and calculated to excite pleasing emotions in the mind of the reader.'[1]

Bewick's wood engravings elevated this hitherto humble skill to both an art form and an industry as wood cuts proved considerably cheaper than engraving in steel or copper and Bewick's skill made up for the previous lack of sharp detail and softness of tone that was achievable in metal. The illustration of books became easier and Bewick himself spawned a school of disciples several of whom became leading artists in their own right: Robert Johnston, Luke Clennell and William Harvey.

Throughout the whole of his long life Bewick maintained his interest in natural history, he never lost his sense of humour and he always strove to pass on his knowledge to the next generation. He is rightly regarded as the father of the art of wood engraving and he is a figure of considerable importance on Tyneside in terms of both industry and art. His career represents the perfect marriage of these two, often widely divergent, disciplines.

[1] *Tyneside Celebrities* William D Lawson, published privately, 1873.

St Nicholas Cathedral (circa 1815).

William Murdoch
1754 - 1839

The man who discovered gas

William Murdoch's fame has largely been obscured by that of his master, James Watt. Recent studies, however, have begun to highlight his own quite crucial and independent role in the development of both the gas and engineering industries. He embodies the combination of a tough and pragmatic personality with entrepreneurial flair and design genius, which so characterised the great out-pouring of talent from Tyneside in the late 18th and early 19th century.

William Murdoch's career is inextricably linked with James Watt, who was his contemporary and employer. Indeed Murdoch was employed by the firm of Boulton & Watt for more than 50 years. Murdoch's admirers now believe that James Watt made fairly free use of Murdoch's inventions and claimed the credit for himself. It appears likely that Watt's celebrated steam pumping-engine could not have been adapted to provide the element of rotative power required to turn the mills and looms of the industrial revolution without Murdoch's sun and planet gear, the design of which was incorporated in Watt's patent.

Watt invented the double acting steam engine, as distinct from Newcomen's atmospheric engine which powered the development, in the late 18th century, of both the cotton and iron industries. The growth of the latter had been substantially restricted by its former dependence upon water power which was needed to work the bellows in the blast furnaces or the great hammers in the forges. When rivers dried up or the water supply was interrupted the hammers fell silent.

Watt's invention of the rotary engine in 1782 removed this dependency on flowing water. As Watt was the inventor, Boulton appears to have been the marketeer though it still took some years before the new engine came into general use.

British Gas

Murdoch developed the steam carriage some two decades before the Cornishman Trevithick, an innovation which seems to have been discouraged, if not actively surpressed, by Watt. Murdoch, however, proved irrepressible and he invented the first steam engine to have an oscillary cylinder which became the basis of all marine engines for the next half-century.

Murdoch was a prolific designer: in the infant machine tool industry he was admired by the great machine tool inventors Maudsley and Naismyth. The firm's workshops in Soho and Birmingham were full of the pneumatic tools, engines and boring machines he invented. Murdoch experimented with pneumatic power and used it to operate the bells on his own front door; until recently, his pneumatic delivery system was in use in Harrod's store in Knightsbridge.

Murdoch's greatest achievement was almost certainly the discovery of gas, the bicentennial of which was celebrated in 1992. His own home was gas-fire heated by ducted warm air. On 13 January 1818 a substantial crowd gathered in Mosley Street to watch the lighting of the first gas lamps which replaced the earlier and much less efficient, oil-filled types. An even larger crowd gathered in 1829 when St. Nicholas' church clock was lighted by gas for the first time.

Although the effect of the Murdoch and Watt steam engine was immediately felt in the cotton and iron industries it took longer to be introduced into the mines. The coal industry was dominated by established practice and was relatively slow to innovate.

Murdoch was a man of considerable physical, as well as mental, talents; in the course of his long life and working career he did not shirk dangers or the call for adventure. When Watt and Boulton retired in 1800 Murdoch remained with the firm as an *eminence grise* to James Watt Jnr. and Matthew Boulton Jnr. He worked actively in the dangerous environment of the Cornish tin mines, installing Boulton and Watt steam engines. He fought verbal and physical battles with tough Cornish mine captains and even led a naval foray to beat off an attack by French privateers threatening to make a prize of the vessel carrying one of his precious engines.

Charles 2nd Earl Grey
1764 - 1845

The man who reformed Parliament

Charles Grey was one of Britain's greatest social reformers, abolishing slavery and promoting greater fairness and democracy. His achievement was particularly remarkable given the age into which he was born.

The years between 1786 and 1832 were crucial to the development of the English political system. Europe was thrown into turmoil by a revolution in France, followed by the long anguish of the Napoleonic Wars. Industrial growth matched agricultural stagnation and there was a great drift of population to the new towns and cities springing up all over England. Living conditions for a new class of industrial workers were almost universally appalling. The revolutionary ideals which crossed the Channel fuelled a new breed of radicalism and the old order was increasingly challenged. Unrest was met by oppression. Measures against treason and sedition were passed, and the Habeas Corpus Act suspended. Regular troops were frequently in evidence culminating in the infamous Peterloo Massacre of 1819 when panicking soldiers charged a threatening crowd.

Charles Grey was destined to play a significant role in this pivotal period. He was born at Falloden in Northumberland though he was educated at a preparatory school in London, and then at Eton where he distinguished himself academically. He went from Eton to Cambridge where his performance was equally brilliant. Upon graduation he accompanied the Duke of Cumberland on the grand tour of Europe, an excursion considered almost obligatory for young gentleman of taste and breeding. In 1786 a vacancy occured in the county of Northumberland and the young Grey, at the age of 22, was elected to Parliament, a seat which he continued to hold for the next two decades.

His maiden speech was such that a Parliamentary colleague, Mr. Addington, who later became Speaker, was moved to say that, 'I do not go too far in declaring that, in the advantage of figure, voice, elocution and manner he is not surpassed by any member of the House'.

Community programme

Grey's Monument 1881 (from a photograph by P. M. Laws).

Early in his political career he defined the style which was to endure throughout. He was by nature and instinct a Liberal. He advocated avoidance of the war with France, opposed the raising of volunteer forces and endeavoured at all times to maintain a pacifist stance. In 1806 when the united parties of Grenville and Fox came to power Grey, (then Lord Howick) was appointed as First Lord of the Admiralty. When Fox died in the following year he was elevated to the rank of Foreign Secretary. Nonetheless his principles were such that, in 1812, he refused to accept a place in the Perceval ministry and was prepared to remain on the back benches until 1830. His repute was still such that, in that year, he was asked to accept the premiership.

The electoral system at this time was manifestly corrupt. The new and spreading industrial cities such as Manchester and Birmingham had scarcely any representation whereas many old or rotten boroughs still returned two or three members. Classic examples were Old Sarum — a long decayed settlement, largely inhabited by sheep which returned two members — and one which had completely disappeared under the North Sea! Yet there was violent Tory opposition to eradicating these inequalities: any element of reform was tainted by the hint of radicalism and was therefore to be opposed at all costs. Undeterred, Grey became the architect of the Great Reform Bill of 1832 — the masterpiece of his political career.

He was also active in promoting the Debtors' Act and the long overdue Catholic Emancipation Bill which was opposed almost as vehemently as the Great Reform Bill. It is difficult, now, to appreciate the strength of feeling aginst the emancipation of Roman Catholics at that time, yet Grey argued all his proposals through with modesty, intelligence and charm. He showed himself to be a man of infinite academic and administrative gifts. The abolition of the slave trade was one of his particular quests. When Foreign Secretary, in 1807, he abolished the trade and formally abolished slavery in 1834.

His philosophy is best summed up by his famous reply to the second reading of the Reform Bill in 1832: 'I had no desire for place, and it was not sought after by me. It was offered to me under such circumstances that nothing but a sense of duty could have induced me to accept it.'

The famous column which bears his name was erected to his honour in 1838. His political career drew to a close when he became ill in 1843. Two years after he died, his remains were interred in Howick Church.

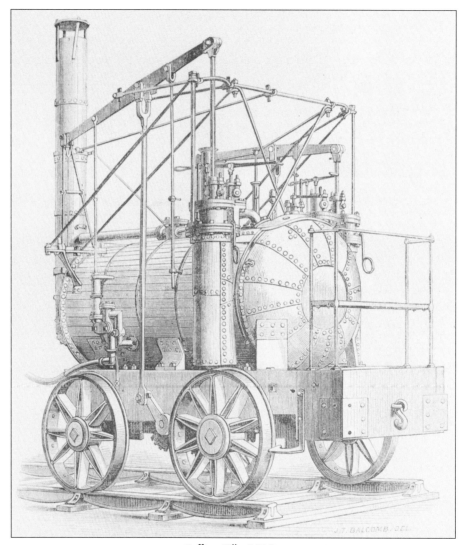

Puffing Billy, 1813.

William Hedley
1779 - 1843

Enter the famous Puffing Billy

While few will have heard of William Hedley, nearly everyone will have heard of *Puffing Billy*, the engine he invented.

Hedley was born toward the end of the 18th century, an era which had seen a major revolution in established coal-mining techniques. From the middle of that century onward, the introduction of the controlled use of gun-powder had facilitated the sinking of ever deeper shafts and the use of cast iron cylinders in place of earlier brass models for larger pumping engines had allowed miners to work the riches of the deeper seams. In 1758 Walker Pit was sunk in the Wallsend basin to a depth of 600 feet and the shaft was drained by no less than three engines.

Deep mining was not without its perils. Explosive gases caused heavy loss of life, and it was not until the introduction of the safety lamp — invented almost simultaneously by both Davy and Stephenson, in 1815 — that the risk of accidents from combustion was reduced.

For some time quantities of coal had been dragged by horses along wooden wagon-ways which were, toward the end of the century, gradually being replaced by iron rails. The first stretch to be laid in Tyneside was that from Walker to the Staithes in 1797. In the declining years of the century the highly innovative Cornish mining engineer Trevithick visited Newcastle and introduced his new steam locomotives to the area.

William Hedley was born at Newburn and educated at Wylam school. At an early age he was appointed a viewer at Walbottle Colliery. Hedley, like his near contemporary Stephenson, demonstrated a considerable natural ability with steam locomotives and in 1813 the owner of Wylam Colliery, Christopher Blackett, commissioned him to design an engine which was intended to carry his coals along the line from Wylam to the staithes at Lemington.

National Westminster Bank PLC

Blackett had, in fact, earlier consulted Trevithick in 1804 and had even gone as far as ordering one of the Cornishman's engines, though he never actually took delivery. One of the reasons for this was that, at that time, the five-mile wagon way was still in timber and the wooden rails had not yet been replaced by iron. When Blackett contacted Trevithick again, the latter was no longer interested in taking his order.

The Cornishman's indifference proved Hedley's opportunity and his engine became famous as the *Puffing Billy*. The design was based loosely upon Trevithick's precedent but, in terms of engineering and design, proved far superior. The new locomotive demonstrated that loads of coal could be moved by the traction of wheels on smooth rails, something which had previously been uncertain.

Although he designed the system which powered *Puffing Billy*, he utilised, but did not perfect, the principle of the blast pipe as a mode of producing greater draft by channelling the exhaust steam into a chimney.

Hedley's innovation was a major link in the chain which, in turn, steered Stephenson to the development of the railway and, as such, it marks a significant advance in the industrial development of Tyneside, and indeed, England as a whole.

William Hedley died aged 64, at Burnhopeside Hall near Lanchester, and lies buried at Newburn.

George Stephenson
1781 - 1848

Father of the industrial revolution

George Stephenson is viewed by many as the father of the industrial revolution on Tyneside. His name is forever linked with that spirit of thrusting genius which refused to be overawed by natural or man-made obstacles and who, despite a lack of formal education, carved out a place for himself both in contemporary society, and in history, by the sheer weight of his genius and personality.

George was the second child of a large family, which existed at barely subsistence level. His father was a humble foreman at Wylam Colliery so the young George did not enjoy the benefits of schooling but, at the age of 14, he was appointed assistant fireman to his father. Soon he rose to become a fireman in his own right and, by the age of 17, had been promoted to Engineman at Waterow Colliery where his father now worked as a fireman under his direction. His early experience as an engineman led him to an intimate knowledge of colliery machinery which would stand him in good stead later on. As a young man, aged 18, Stephenson could still neither read nor write. Nonetheless, with single-minded determination, he set to work on a drastic course of academic self-improvement and very soon had mastered not only the literary arts, but also science and mathematics.

By 1810, he was a brakesman at Killingworth: it was the year Killingworth High Pit was sunk. This ambitious project came close to being thwarted because the pumping engines available could not cope. The owners called in a series of experts who were unable to propose any effective solution and when these had failed, they allowed Stephenson, largely out of desperation, to try his hand. In four days he had stripped, modified and rebuilt the existing engine to a specification adequate to withstand the increased demand. This was the birth of the Stephenson legend: his immediate reward was to be promoted to engineman at Killingworth at the then considerable salary of £100 a year. His reputation as a worker of miracles with colliery engines began to spread.

Community Unit

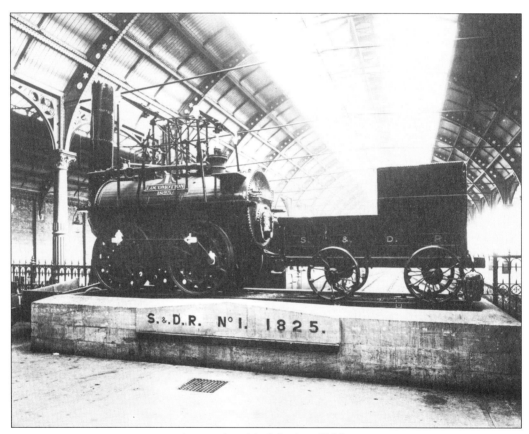

Locomotion. No 1 Engine, 1825.

Very soon he had moved on from the science of engines to study locomotion by steam power. His first design, completed in 1815, and backed by Lord Ravensworth was unsuccessful, but his second was more promising. Stephenson had as his goal a universal railway system. It is difficult to appreciate now how great a leap in the public perception this was: contemporary engineers were sceptical, land owners outraged and Parliament perplexed. So great was the furore generated by Stephenson's ideas that a full Parliamentary enquiry was held and the blunt Northumbrian engineer found himself faced by a battery of eight or ten of the country's finest barristers. Nonetheless he refused to be overawed and, after much debate, his enthusiasm and his skill won the day.

In 1821 he was appointed as engineer to the Stockton & Darlington Railway at the enormous salary of £300 a year. The original line ran from Whitton Park Colliery, near Bishop Auckland, through Darlington to Stockton, a distance of some 25 miles. Having been authorised by Parliament in 1821 it was formally opened on 27 September 1825.

The initial success of the Stockton and Darlington line led to the development of a second stretch of track between Liverpool and Manchester and, within a further two years, an additional 300 miles of track had been laid. Stephenson was the man of the hour.

In the June of 1823 Stephenson and his son Robert, with Edward Pease of Darlington and Michael Longridge of the Bedlington Iron Works, formed a new company to make locomotives and, early in 1824, set up their workshop on Forth Street, behind what is now the Central Station.

The first locomotives were disappointing. Although, on the opening day of the Stockton to Darlington, 450 passengers and a load of coal had been carried to Darlington at speeds of 12 miles per hour, the early engines proved less than reliable. The prototype models built in Stephenson's workshops were not particularly successful. The future of steam locomotion was in doubt until, in 1827, Timothy Hackworth designed and built *The Royal George* which represented a significant and much needed technical advance. Then, in 1829, Stephenson more than compensated for the disappointment of his earlier models by producing his masterpiece — the famous *Rocket*. This design coupled an engine with a multi-tubular boiler to a powerful steam blast recovery and achieved the then unheard of speed of 36 miles per hour.

Although Stephenson cannot claim the credit for actually having invented the locomotive, he brought about the fundamental alliance of the locomotive and the railway system which changed the face of Victorian Britain throughout the latter half of the 19th century. He was effectively the founder of the iron railways which, within a generation, were to transform not just Britain but the whole of western Europe.

Central Station, Newcastle upon Tyne (John Dobson, 1850).

John Dobson
1787 - 1854

The man who shaped Newcastle

Dobson, long regarded as Tyneside's architectural genius, was himself a pupil of the talented David Stephenson who was responsible for the construction of Dean Street in the late 18th century and is particularly remembered for his very fine church of All Saints. The young Dobson therefore received a grounding in the classical style, which he was to make his own, and was also fired by a sense of civic pride coupled with an awareness of opportunity. The city was particularly fortunate that Dobson's design and architectural flair would be linked to the thrusting entrepreneurial talents of Richard Grainger.

Amongst his earliest commissions were the police station and gaol in Carliol Square. He completed the station itself in 1831 and the gaol in 1834. Prior to this, he had designed the chapels and gateways for Jesmond Road cemetery in 1824. He was in fact quite active in the sphere of religious buildings and two years after he had completed the design for Jesmond Road cemetery he planned St. James' chapel in Blackett Street for the Presbyterian Church. In 1854, he designed the Church of Divine Unity in Newbridge Street and, perhaps his most famous religious monument, the church of St. Thomas the Martyr in Barras Bridge, was built to his plans and consecrated in 1830, the year in which the old church of the same name was pulled down to widen the entry into Sandhill.

Richard Grainger was a builder by trade and came from humble origins, his father being a quayside porter. A decade before he entered into partnership with Grainger, Dobson had proposed to the civic fathers a bold scheme to rebuild completely 12 acres of essentially derelict property which covered an area from the top of Pilgrim Street to St. Andrews. Grainger subsequently bought the site and it was the potent mix of his persuasive tenacity and Dobson's visionary planning, perhaps helped by Clayton's influence, which secured the backing of the city for their great scheme of redevelopment.

The result was the building of Grey Street, Grainger Street and Clayton Street which gave direct communication to the lower town whilst lateral communications were provided by Hood Street, Shakespeare Street, Market Street, Nunn Street and Nelson Street. The triangle created by Market Street, Grainger Street and Grey Street enclosed the Central Exchange which, as the Corporation declined to use it as a corn market, was opened as a subscription newsroom. The fine sweep of Grey Street was broken only by the projecting portico of the new Theatre Royal, which was not in fact built to Dobson's plan but to one propounded by Benjamin Green. Grey Street is certainly Dobson's finest achievement in civic design. Few, if any, provincial towns can boast of such sweeping majesty and few cities have benefited from such a comprehensive and inspired redesign of the urban core.

It is all the more remarkable that the Dobson/Grainger scheme has remained virtually intact in the 150 years since its construction and was of sufficient importance to withstand the ravages of the city planners who wreaked such havoc in the 1960s.

Dobson did not confine his restless energies to the purely classical, however. He was an early pioneer in the design of commercial and industrial buildings. When the High Level Bridge was constructed in 1849 utilising some 5,000 tons of cast and wrought iron, Dobson provided a perfect architectural riposte with his superb Central Station, opened by Queen Victoria in August 1850.

Dobson and Grainger were responsible for moving the axis of the city's commercial orientation away from the Quayside toward the upper levels of Grey Street and Grainger Street. In 1837 the Mansion House in The Close was sold by the Corporation and the gaggle of existing buildings was demolished to provide clearer and better access. The building of the Corn Exchange and Town Hall in 1858 beside the Keep was heartily disapproved of by both Dobson and Grainger who thought that a site of their own choosing between Market Street and Blackett Street would have been far more appropriate.

Dobson's association with the rise of Tyneside was further evidenced by the number of country house commissions he undertook. He applied his classical knowledge to assist Monck Middleton in the building of Belsay Hall (1810-1817) and he built further houses in the classical tradition at Nunnykirk in 1825, Meldon in 1832, and also at Mitford and Longhirst. He branched, with considerable success into the gothic style with Beaufront overlooking the Tyne Valley which was built between 1837 and 1841. A third style involved the grand Tudor manner with which he experimented at Lilburn Tower, (1828-1843).

Dobson was a prolific as well as a highly-skilled practitioner and Tyneside is indeed fortunate that a man destined to make such a strong visual impact upon its city and landscape should have possessed such prodigious talent.

Robert Hawthorn
1796 - 1867

From an open shed to world renown

Robert Hawthorn is one of the towering figures of the industrial revolution. It was a momentous day for Tyneside when, in the January of 1817, he founded an engineering works on Forth Banks.

Like so many of his contemporaries his background was in coal-mining — his father had been an engineer at Walbottle Colliery for some 50 years. Initially his business was a small concern with only four employees, all of the machinery operated by hand-wheel and the premises consisting of an open shed on the west side of Forth Banks. Nonetheless, the business soon began to develop; in 1819, Hawthorn bought an adjoining piece of land on which, with the aid of his workforce then numbering 20, he constructed a new purpose-built workshop. The building work was carried out in the evenings, after working hours, so as not to damage productivity. As the firm continued to expand, in 1820, he was joined by his brother William forming a partnership.

Initially Hawthorn manufactured general machinery for saw mills, corn mills and collieries. By 1822 steam power had been introduced to the works and, from 1824 onward, he began to manufacture small marine engines. Five years later he built his first road traction engine of, by contemporary standards, a hefty six horsepower. Over the next 40 years, the Hawthorn Works turned out over 1,000 steam locomotives and, after the launch of the *John Bowes* in 1852, he began to specialise in the manufacture of marine engines for the new breed of iron ships.

Even before the building of the *John Bowes* the firm had made an engine for a Wallsend-built iron ship, the *QED,* which was the earliest sailing collier to use auxiliary steam and was the first vessel fitted with a double bottom for water balance.

Robert Hawthorn, founder of the business, died in 1867 and his brother William retired in 1870. With

TYNE

WEAR

DEVELOPMENT
CORPORATION

Forth Banks, (circa 1900).

the passing of this era the business was restructured and the directors bought up the shipyard of T.&W. Smith at St. Peter's Basin. In 1885 the business amalgamated with Leslie & Co. Limited to form R.&W. Hawthorn Leslie & Co. Ltd, one of the great industrial names of Tyneside.

Hawthorn Leslie maintained a steady contribution toward the development of shipbuilding technique and twice in the 19th century pioneered innovative forms of construction, firstly in the transition from sail to steam and, 50 years later, in the change from reciprocating engines to turbines. In 1899 the company made the hull and boilers for the turbine destroyer *Viper* to Parson's design. By the outbreak of the First World War in 1914, the firm's locomotives, marine engines and ships had won world renown — a far cry from the open shed of a century earlier.

Tin advertisement for Fairy soap.

Thomas Hedley
1802 - 1877

Success in the form of soap

Tyneside's most famous brand is probably Fairy soap. The man behind it was Thomas Hedley.

Hedley was born at Harnham, a bleak mid-Northumberland farmhouse and a former border fortress perched high upon a rocky outcrop. The farm where Hedley grew up was formerly the home of a famous beauty Catherine Babbington — known as Kate O'Harnham — who flouted Puritan convention during the days of the Protectorate to such a degree that her body was denied burial in consecrated ground and rested for many years in a domestic sepulchre below the crag.

Thomas Hedley was apprenticed as an assistant to the firm of John Greene & Son of Gateshead who were general grocers and ships chandlers. Later, he joined Nichol and Ludlow, a firm of Newcastle ship owners. But, in 1840, he rejoined his former master, John Greene, as a partner to establish a new soap-works on Tyneside.   Hedley subsequently bought out Greene and, until his death, the firm traded as Thomas Hedley & Co.

Throughout the 19th century, the firm grew and prospered and Hedley became a leading civic figure on Tyneside: he was elected mayor in 1863. In 1880, he became chairman of the Tyne Steam Shipping Co. of Willington Quay. He was also a director of the Consett Iron Works and chairman of the Newcastle & Gateshead Gas Co.

The soap industry managed to avoid the decline of the Tyneside chemical industry in the middle and last quarters of the 19th century, though, by 1900 only the firms of Hedley and Taylor remained. Soap manufacture was related to the alkaline industry in that the process involved the use of alkali fat whereas other industries, such as glass, relied on alkali sand and lime.

Procter &Gamble

39

The chemical industry was one of the earliest industrial processes to be developed on Tyneside. William Losh & Partners began to make soda at Walker in 1796 and within 20 years copperas—or green vitriol— was being manufactured at Felling, cold tar, sal ammoniac and trussiate of iron at Heworth, and oil of vitriol at Bill Quay and Walker.

In the latter part of the 19th century, the chemical industry was constrained by the rapid development of the three staples—coal, shipbuilding and engineering. From 1850 onward the impetus for development shifted to Teesside. At one point, the celebrated radical Thomas Doubleday was a partner for Whig Anthony Easterby in a soap business located in The Close.

Given the famous advertising associated with the Fairy brand, it is ironic that in the 1890s Hedley's were boasting that they relied upon quality rather than upon advertising. By the turn of the century this policy had been reversed as the firm began to rely increasingly on the power of advertising and promotion. As the 19th century neared its end, production had increased dramatically and the firm was relying on a wide range of imported raw materials particularly African palm oil used extensively after 1890. By 1898 the firm was setting aside money to fund its advertising budget and Fairy soap was the first product to be heavily promoted.

The recession which followed the end of the First World War in 1918 had a catastrophic effect on Tyneside and by the late 1920s, Hedley's was in deep financial difficulties. A white knight arrived in the form of the American firm Procter & Gamble, based in Cincinatti. The merger took place in 1930 and the increased American influence and resources spawned a new range of products all of which were promoted by skilful and sustained advertising; Oxydol in 1930, Sylvan Flakes in 1933 and Mirro in 1934.

Today, Procter & Gamble remains as one of the great names of Tyneside and continues to thrive: the soap manufacturer which was at one time threatened by the growth of the main staples has in fact outstripped and outlasted them all.

Note: Thomas Hedley is to be differentiated from another Hedley of the same name, who was the son of William Hedley, the engineer and who is now chiefly remembered for his gift of Benwell Towers as a residence for the Bishop of Newcastle.

William Armstrong
1810 - 1900

Bringer of the big guns

William Armstrong was the son of alderman William Armstrong, a successful corn merchant, and his boyhood home was in Shieldfield on a site subsequently covered by the former LNER Goods Station. Initially he was directed toward a career in the professions and, after qualifying as a solicitor, engaged in private practice for 12 years. Throughout this period, however, he maintained a keen interest in engineering and, in 1844, he lectured to a capacity crowd at the Literary and Philosophical Society. His interest and enthusiasm won him election as a member of the Royal Society. On a more mercantile basis, he was already attracting support from a consortium of local investors including his law partner Armourer Duncan.

In 1846 he undertook his first practical project when he sought to convert the existing cranes on Newcastle Quayside to operate by hydraulic pressure. This initial experiment was a success and, together with his backers, he formed the Newcastle Cranage Company. Initially most of the engineering work was sub-contracted to Watson's Engineering Works in High Bridge Street but, early in 1847, Armstrong made undoubtedly the most important decision of his life, when he quit his solicitor's desk for good and, in the summer of that year, bought five and a half acres in the once-quiet village of Elswick upon which to build his own factory.

The new factory prospered and a rush of orders came in for machinery to service docks, railways and mines. This purely commercial trade was boosted by the Crimean War which raged between 1854-56. The carnage and horror of this campaign provided an opportunity for an entrepreneurial designer of Armstrong's stamp. In 1855 he invented a new type of breech loading and rifled field piece. This weapon revolutionised the science of artillery and large numbers were sold to the British Army and later to the Union forces during the American Civil War of 1861-65. Whereas nowadays, we may, have doubts about the morality of arms manufacture, there can be little doubt that the Armstrong gun

NORTHUMBRIAN WATER GROUP PLC

contributed enormously to the wealth and success of Tyneside as a manufacturing economy and, in so doing, provided work for thousands. Three years after the cessation of hostilities in the Crimea, Armstrong secured his knighthood by giving the patents for the gun to the government and entering into a joint venture known as the Elswick Ordnance Company. Subsequently, however, he severed his connection with the government and, in 1863, merged his engineering and arms businesses. Throughout the rest of the century guns manufactured on Tyneside saw action around the globe.

In 1868, Armstrong diversified into naval warships and built his first gunboat for the Admiralty. The vessel was actually built to order in the Walker Yard of C.W. Mitchell. The success of the venture prompted Armstrong to suggest a merger and, in 1882, the two companies amalgamated as WG Armstrong Mitchell & Co. So successful was the new company that a yard specifically built to accommodate the construction of warships was opened at Elswick and the Walker yard continued to supply mainly merchant shipping.

Once the founder had passed his 70th birthday he gradually divested himself of day-to-day interest in the business and left the running of the company in the capable hands of his former deputies. These included Sir Andrew Noble, Colonel H.F. Swan, G.W. Rendel and P.G.B. Westmacott. In 1884, the firm expanded once again by opening a steel works and, in 1897, it acquired the armaments firm Sir Joseph Whitworth, the new amalgamated business now bearing the famous name of Armstrong Whitworth & Co.

The business prospered in the hands of Armstrong's successors. Noble contributed to the development of armaments and Swan developed the basis of the modern oil tanker. Rendel was an experienced naval architect and it was under his supervision that the majority of the Japanese fleet, which defeated the Russians at Tsushima in 1905, was constructed on Tyneside.

Armstrong, in his later years, did not hesitate to share the great wealth which he had amassed. He contributed extensively to the movement toward creating open spaces in the urban landscape and, in 1880, gave to the Corporation the nucleus of the park now named after him and, three years later, he made a further gift of Jesmond Dene and the Banqueting Hall.

He retired to his country seat of Cragside which he built in rolling hill country near Rothbury in mid-Northumberland, the house designed by the leading architect Norman Shaw. Although the building was traditional in construction Armstrong installed an electricity supply fuelled by a water turbine and thus Cragside became the first large country house in England to have electric light and appliances.

When Armstrong died, in 1900 his original 5.5 acre site in Elswick had grown to 230 acres, the workforce numbered 25,000 and the thunder of his guns was heard on every battlefield.

Sir Joseph Wilson Swan
1828 - 1914

An electrifying moment for Newcastle

In 1879, some three years after Graham Bell had invented the telephone, Joseph Wilson Swan, in his home laboratory at Underhill in Gateshead, invented the incandescent lamp almost simultaneously with Edison in the United States.

In the following year he was able to provide electric illumination to his premises, Swan & Morgan, and subsequently to the whole of Mosley Street. Thus Newcastle became the first city in Britain with electric light.

Like many Tyneside entrepreneurs Swan did not enjoy the full benefit of a formal education. Born at Pallion Hall in Sunderland, he attended Hendon Lodge School, but left at the age of 13. Later he was to say: 'I think it was not so much what I learnt at school as what I spontaneously absorbed out of school by keeping my eyes and ears wide open.'

He resided briefly on Teesside but soon returned to his native Wear where, in 1842, he began a six-year apprenticeship with the chemists, Hudson and Osbaldiston. A lecture given by one W.E. Swaite at the Sunderland Athenaeum in 1845 on the subject of electric light fuelled what was to become his life-long passion.

He was released from his apprenticeship by the untimely deaths of both partners and left Wearside to join his brother-in-law John Mawson, also a chemist, in Newcastle. Mawson was something of a civic figure and later became High Sheriff. He had established a circle of liberal, free-minded scientists of which Swan soon became an accepted member. This widening of his horizons produced a brief flirtation with politics and he became a member of the Liberal Party, even going so far as to bring out a short-lived political broad sheet.

NORTHERN ELECTRIC

Northern Electric

In 1862, he married his first wife, Fanny, in London and moved into 21 Leazes Terrace, Newcastle. Some five years later Mawson was tragically killed whilst trying to dispose of some nitro-glycerine. Shortly after this blow, Swan's loss was compounded by the death of Fanny and two of his sons. The grieving widower, unable to bear the memories of his house in Leazes Terrace, moved his surviving family to Gateshead. Some time after, he formed an attachment to his sister-in-law, Hannah, whom he eventually married in 1871 though, due to restrictions imposed by English law, the marriage had to take place in Switzerland.

In 1881, Swan together with Armstrong, Spence, Watson and J.T. Merz, formed Swan's Electric Light Company Ltd and opened a factory in South Benwell, the first in Europe to manufacture the complete electric lamp. So successful was the business that Swan felt the need to move the company's head office from its established Mosley Street base to London and the factory was moved from Benwell to Ponders End in Middlesex.

The new electrical industry with which Swan's name will for ever be inextricably linked formed one of the cornerstones of Tyneside's industrial greatness and, though the latter part of his life was spent in the south, there is no doubt that his heart always remained within the North. It was here that his creative talent first found expression and it was Tyneside and the North which proved his true and lasting beneficiaries.

Sir George Burton Hunter

1845 - 1937

Launching a shipbuilding giant

The name of Sir George Burton Hunter is linked with shipbuilding and marine engineering, on Tyneside, through the great Swan Hunter shipyard. He left school at 13 to begin an apprenticeship to Thomas Meek, the river commissioner's engineer. He moved from this employment to join W. Pile, Hay & Co. and, by 1871, he was in charge of their drawing office. After a brief sojourn in Scotland he returned to Pile's as manager and two years later, on the death of William Pile, he became a junior partner to S.P. Austin whose company was renamed Austin & Hunter. In 1872, C.S. Swan, who had owned and managed a shipyard at Wallsend, died and Hunter was quick to develop a relationship and form a new partnership with Swan's widow. This firm was to bear the now famous name of C.S. Swan and Hunter.

In 1860, a contemporary of Hunter, John Wigham Richardson, bought the shipyard at Low Walker from which Messrs. Cutts had, some 18 years previously, launched the first iron ship to be built on the Tyne. The area of this new yard which the owner called the Neptune Works covered some four acres with a river frontage of a mere 107 yards. It had only three building slips, the longest of which was no more than 320 feet. Nevertheless, it provided employment for 200 people and was able to produce 4,000 gross tons of shipping a year.

In the same year as Hunter slipped neatly into the vacuum left by Swan, Richardson set up the Neptune engineering works and, in 1898, the shipyard was enlarged by the formation of the new north yard. Adjoining the Neptune works and somewhat further down the river were the premises of the Tyne Pontoon and Dry Dock Company which was established in 1882 and provided dry docking and ship preparing facilities. Next to this yard was that of C.S. Swan & Hunter.

In 1903 a significant merger took place when Wigham Richardson and Swan Hunter amalgamated

ACTION FOR CITIES

45

and together bought the Tyne Pontoon and Dry Dock Company yard. The total area available to the new company now comprised some 78 acres and had a full 4,000 feet of river frontage.

Firmly committed to expansion, the new company consolidated its position by securing a controlling interest in the Wallsend Slipway and Engineering Company whose works covered a further 53 acres to the east of the Wallsend Slipway. In 1912, the company further expanded its operation on a national basis by acquiring the engineering works of Barclay Curle & Co. Ltd from Glasgow whose substantial Clydeside yards produced 70,000 tons of shipping a year.

In the decade between 1903 and 1913 the yard averaged an output of some 93,000 tons a year. Ships were built on 17 slips which were serviced by electrically-powered overhead cranes. One of the great high points in the yard's history came in 1907 with the launching of the Cunard Liner *Mauretania*. In its day this was the biggest and fastest vessel in the world; its construction was an extremely prestigious order for Tyneside. She carried 2,335 passengers with a crew of 812, driven by four propellers powered by Parson's steam turbines with a 70,000 horsepower output. Her sister ship was the ill-fated *Lusitania*, torpedoed by a German U-boat in 1915 with a great loss of life. Nonetheless the *Mauretania* continued to ply the Atlantic for over two decades and later served as a troop ship.

Like many other Tyneside concerns, the First World War produced a spate of orders for warships and, in 1914-1918, Swan Hunter produced 55 warships with a gross weight of 100,000 tons plus an additional 290,000 gross tons of merchant shipping.

John Holmes
1857 - 1935

Switching on the power

John Holmes was a pioneer in the field of electricity and it is, in many ways, unfair that his fame has been eclipsed by that of his contemporary Swan. He was, nonetheless, one of the great innovators and craftsmen of electrical design. In the summer of 1883, he installed electric lighting at his father's house, Welburn in Jesmond, the first private dwelling to benefit from electric light in the city. The new form of illumination proved something of a sensation and Holmes' experiment generated a rush of orders.

One such was the installation of electric lighting at the new Wallsend Cafe, and it was whilst working on this project that Holmes suffered a minor accident the nature of which suggested to him the idea for the original quick-break switch. The switch with snap-off action was patented by him the following year and, in 1885, he made his first dynamo, the Castle, one of the earliest in the country and one which proved extremely successful.

He pioneered the development of train-lighting sets, electric-drive mechanisms for printing presses and supplied the portable lighting sets used on the Suez Canal for night navigation. He was a particularly skilled and meticulous craftsman and made most of his prototypes himself in his own workshop. After his death, in 1935, the entire contents were presented by his sister to the Science and Industry Museum.

Prior to this, in 1928, his firm J.H. Holmes & Co. had amalgamated with A. Reyrolle & Co. Ltd. The history of A.C. Reyrolle had also begun in the 1880s when A.C. Reyrolle established a switch gear workshop in London with some employees. By 1901 the business had grown, became incorporated and transferred to Hebburn on Tyne where it occupied a site of 5.5 acres and employed 58 people. As Reyrolles grew, the site extended to some 101 acres and the workforce swelled to 7,000.

TYNE

WEAR

DEVELOPMENT CORPORATION

Reyrolle specialised in the production of switchgear and the company originated the principle of totally enclosing all electrical conductors in metal to provide additional safety. The product list extended to welding sets, electric motors, precision electrical instruments, electrical control equipment for mines, printing presses and ship production.

The electric motors and electric-drive mechanisms for printing presses developed from the prototypes devised by J.H. Holmes whose genius skill and craftsmanship gave Tyneside a significant head start as a centre for excellence in electrical design.

Bibliography

1.   Bates, C.J. — "History of Northumberland" (1894)
2.   Brown, The Rev. H. — "The History of Newcastle upon Tyne" (1736)
3.   Charleton, R.J. — "The History of Newcastle upon Tyne" (1894)
4.   Dougan, D.J. — "The History of North East Shipbuilding" (1968)
5.   Fraser, C.M. and K.Emsley — "Tyneside" (1973)
6.   Heppell, L.W. — "History of Northumberland" (1976)
7.   Hodgson, The Rev. J. — "A Picture of Newcastle upon Tyne" (1812)
8.   Honeyman, H.L. — "Northumberland" (1949)
9.   Horsley, P.M. — "Eighteenth Century Newcastle" (1971)
10. Middlebrook, S. — "Newcastle upon Tyne" (1950)
11. Tomlinson, W.W. — "Comprehensive Guide to the County of Northumberland" (1863)